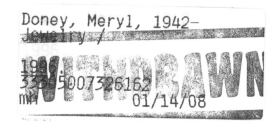

JEWELRY

Meryl Doney

FRANKLIN WATTS
A Division of Grolier Publishing
LONDON • NEW YORK • HONG KONG • SYDNEY
DANBURY, CONNECTICUT

About this book

You may think that jewelry is just expensive decoration for rich people. That's not true at all! An enormous number and variety of personal decorations are made and worn by people all over the world. And it's not only girls and women who wear jewelry. In some cultures men are the most beautifully adorned.

As you will discover in this book, different cultures have developed their own distinctive styles of decoration. Many have also swapped or traded beads from other areas of the world to add to their own tradition of jewelry.

In this book you will find examples of jewelry made by many different peoples. Maps will show you which country or part of the world each item comes from.

The jewelry shown here represents only a tiny part of the rich variety in the world. If you want to learn more about jewelry, try to find some of the books listed on page 30. As you begin to know what to look for, you can search for unusual items of jewelry in thrift shops, sales, or even the family attic.

This book contains many different methods for making your own jewelry. Most of the steps are easy to follow, but where you see this sign ask for help from an adult.

If you want to show off your work, there are instructions for making a board to display it on. You may also like to make items of jewelry for others, to give as gifts or to sell at local fund-raising or charity events.

© 1996 Franklin Watts
Text © 1996 Meryl Doney

First American Edition 1996 by
Franklin Watts
A Division of Grolier Publishing
Sherman Turnpike
Danbury, Connecticut 06816

Series editor: Kyla Barber
Editor: Jane Walker
Design: Visual Image
Cover design: Kirstie Billingham
Artwork: Ruth Levy
Photography: Peter Millard

Library of Congress Cataloging-in-Publication Data

Doney, Meryl, 1942–
    Jewelry/Meryl Doney.
    p.   cm.
    Includes bibliographical references and index.
    Summary: Describes examples of jewelry from around the world, from Italian trading beads to a Chinese hair ornament, and provides instructions for making them yourself.
    ISBN 0-531-14406-2
    1. Jewelry making—Juvenile literature. [1. Jewelry.   2. Jewelry making.   3. Handicraft.]   I. Title.
    TT212.D66 1996
    745.594'2—dc20   95-2056713

                                                              CIP AC

Printed in Great Britain

Contents

A history of jewelry

Any natural object with an unusual color or shape, or with a hole in it, was used to make the earliest jewelry. The object, perhaps a shell, was attached to a thin strip of animal hide and worn as decoration.

In some parts of the world, people make jewelry from the most valuable materials they can afford. They wear the items all the time in order to keep their wealth with them. Jewelry can also demonstrate how important a person you are, which tribe you belong to, and whether you are married or not.

In some cultures jewelry is worn to bring good luck or to scare away evil spirits. Blue and white eye beads made from glass are supposed to protect against the evil eye. In Asia, beads are scattered over crops to bring a good harvest. A bead is thrown into the wedding cup at marriage ceremonies in the Philippines. Beads can also have a religious use (see page 26).

The earliest traders used beads as currency. Large quantities of beads from Europe found their way to Africa, Asia, and the Americas. The jewelry that the local people made with those beads is now a source of inspiration for many jewelers in Europe.

Your own jewelry-making kit

Jewelry makers are always looking for rare or unusual items to include in their work. Try local thrift shops, yard sales, or street fairs; you never know what you might find. You only need a few good tools and a little equipment to make most of the jewelry in this book. Here is a list of the most useful items for your jewelry-making kit:

small hammer • small jeweler's saw • vise • awl • hand drill with small bits • round-nosed pliers • snipe pliers • flat-nosed pliers • wire cutters • tin snips • scissors • craft knife • metal ruler • brushes • gesso • white enamel paint •

poster paints • felt-tip pens • clear nail polish • white glue • tube of strong glue • plastic and bakeable modeling material (polymer clay) • self-hardening modeling clay • masking tape • bead threading tray (see page 29)

Needles

A **beading** needle is fine and flexible, with a small eye.

A **sewing** needle is the most common type of needle.

A **crewel** needle has a long eye for use with embroidery silks.

A **tapestry** needle is blunt with a big eye.

For the finest beads make a needle from a short length of thin copper wire. Bend the wire in half and twist ends together.

Threads

Silk thread is best for beads with small holes.

To use it without a needle, stiffen the end with glue or nail polish.

Nylon thread is fine and can be used double. It is best for light plastic, wood, ceramic, and glass beads.

Nylon monofilament or **fishing line** is very strong, but it is not suitable for metal beads.

Tiger tail is a nylon-coated steel wire for use with heavy or sharp beads.

Elastic thread can be bought in different colors, including gold and silver.

Laces made from cotton or leather are ideal for beads with large holes.

When working out how much thread you need, always add on half as much again to attach fasteners and to tie knots.

Wire

Copper, **brass**, and **silver** wire can be bought in thicknesses, or gauges, with different bending properties. The most useful size of wire is 0.6 mm. You can make a heavier bangle with 1.5-mm wire.

Findings

Many specially made clasps and rings for finishing jewelry can be bought in bead and craft shops. Ethnic jewelry is often finished in very simple ways. Here are some examples:

• button and hole

• knot and loop

• wire hook and ring

• tied strings or leather thongs

Anything available

Everyday objects like seeds and grasses, feathers, shells, and animal bones were some of the first sources of simple jewelry. Most of these are still used today. This necklace on the left is from Papua New Guinea. It is made from threaded shark's teeth. Animal bones, hair, or teeth are often worn to display the power of the hunter who has caught them. In some countries in the past, human bones were worn to demonstrate the wearer's power over his enemies.

The long necklace below is made from a different kind of everyday object. The long thin beads are pieces of broken clay pipe from the nineteenth century. They were found on the shore of the Thames River in London.

Make a seashore necklace

Use anything you like to make your jewelry: beautifully colored feathers, animal teeth, patterned shells, or various seeds and spices. You could make a pair of earrings by threading cloves, dried chili peppers, and star anise (found in spice section) onto strong cotton. The necklace shown here is made from items picked up along the seashore.

You will need: a tray (see page 29) • a collection of interesting objects • beads • plastic modeling material • hand drill and smallest bit • 0.8-mm silver wire • metal rod • wire cutters • pliers • metal file • scissors • silk and needle or tiger tail • wire hook and ring fastener (see page 5)

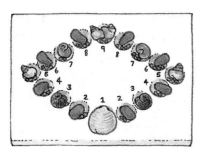

1 Lay out your main items in the tray so that they look attractive. To complete the pattern, drop a few small beads into each bowl of the tray.

2 To pierce shells, press them into plastic modeling material. Position drill bit near the edge and drill carefully. (Some shells may break.)

3 Make silver rings by winding wire around a metal rod several times. Snip each ring with wire cutters.

Thread a bead onto each ring, slip it through shell hole and close.

4 To hold odd-shaped pieces of glass, use pliers to make a loop of silver wire. Lay the glass against the wire with the loop at the top. Wind the wire around the glass from the bottom up, finishing around the loop. Snip end off wire and smooth with a file.

5 Cut a length of silk longer (by half) than you need. Thread through several beads. Turn around hook loop several times and tie in a knot. Thread back through same beads to begin necklace.

6 Thread beads, shells, and glass onto silk. Finish by looping around ring several times and knotting silk. Thread end back through several beads and cut off.

Trading beads

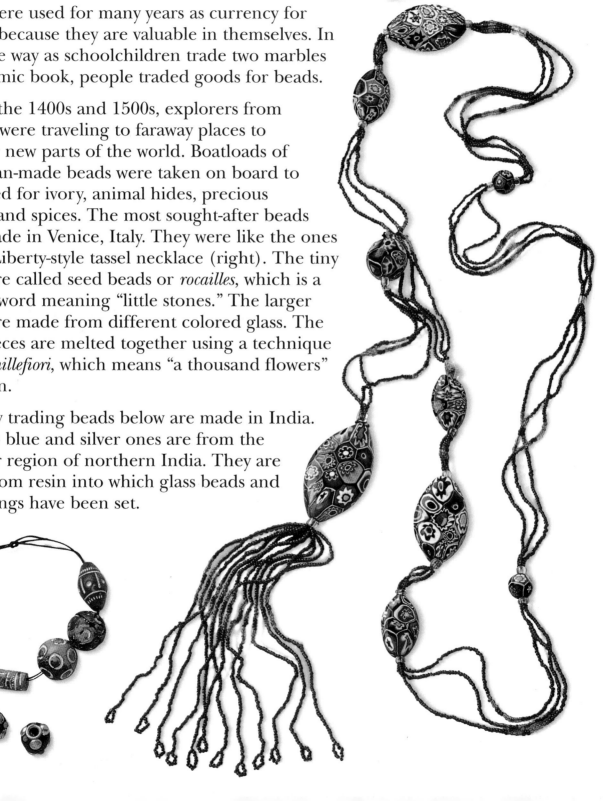

Beads were used for many years as currency for trading because they are valuable in themselves. In the same way as schoolchildren trade two marbles for a comic book, people traded goods for beads.

During the 1400s and 1500s, explorers from Europe were traveling to faraway places to discover new parts of the world. Boatloads of European-made beads were taken on board to be traded for ivory, animal hides, precious metals, and spices. The most sought-after beads were made in Venice, Italy. They were like the ones in this Liberty-style tassel necklace (right). The tiny beads are called seed beads or *rocailles*, which is a French word meaning "little stones." The larger beads are made from different colored glass. The glass pieces are melted together using a technique called *millefiori*, which means "a thousand flowers" in Italian.

The clay trading beads below are made in India. The two blue and silver ones are from the Kashmir region of northern India. They are made from resin into which glass beads and metal rings have been set.

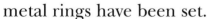

Design your own trading beads

Beads are made from a variety of materials including glass, wood, metal, clay, plastic, precious and semi-precious stones, and other natural objects. Here is a method of making the colorful *millefiori* beads.

You will need: bakeable plastic modeling material (several colors) • craft knife • needle • thread • silver wire • safety pin • cotton fabric • oven

1 Carefully read the safety instructions for the modeling material. Prepare several colors by kneading material. Form small pieces into thin cylinder shapes about 2.5 inches (7 cm) long.

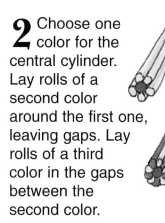

2 Choose one color for the central cylinder. Lay rolls of a second color around the first one, leaving gaps. Lay rolls of a third color in the gaps between the second color.

3 Roll a thin layer of modeling material into a large rectangle. Wrap it around the whole cylinder.

With your fingers, roll the cylinder again until it is long and thin. Cut very thin slices from the cylinder with a craft knife.

4 Form more modeling material into a ball a little smaller than the bead you want to make. Press thin slices from the cylinder all over the surface of the ball. Roll the whole ball in your hands until it is shaped and smooth.

5 Make a hole through the center with a needle. For earrings, make a hole in one edge. Repeat as many times as you want, using other colors and forming different shapes.

6 Bake the material according to instructions. String necklace. Glue silver wire rings into earrings for findings. Attach a safety pin to the back of the brooch by gluing a piece of fabric across it.

MOROCCO
Metals and colored glass

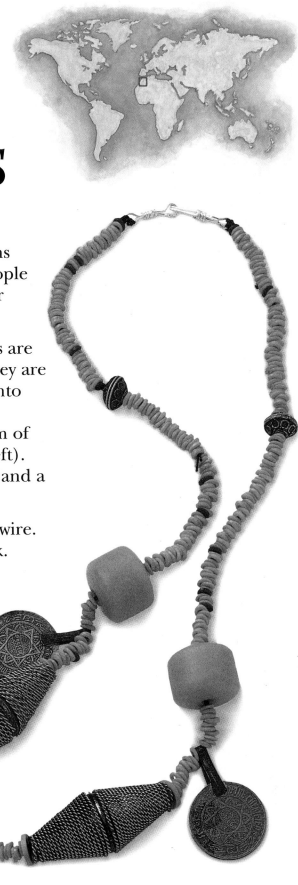

Since earliest times, silversmiths and goldsmiths have made decorations for people to wear. People used the gold and silver items to show off their wealth or to make sure that it was secure.

In some countries where these precious metals are not mined, coins are used to make jewelry. They are melted down and the metal is either formed into ingots to be shaped or it is poured into molds. Money itself is also worn as jewelry, in the form of pierced coins like this 10-franc piece (below left). Moroccan smiths have added a cut-glass stone and a metal hanging ring to the coin.

Moroccan jewelry often features twisted silver wire. This type of work is called filigree or ropework. Throughout the Islamic world, silver is the preferred metal because it is thought to be pure and lucky. The traditional green, yellow, and blue colors on the silver pendant shown right have been added by using enamel. This is a kind of colored glass that is melted onto the surface at a high temperature.

Make your own plastic enamel

Real enameling is a very complex process. However, you can copy the idea by using the plastic granules that are sold with kits for making stained glass-effect pictures. Here are examples of pendants, earrings, and a ring made in this way.

You will need: 0.8-mm silver wire • wire cutters • vise • small metal eyelet or hook • hand drill • aluminum foil, cut from pie tin • pencil • scissors • plastic granules • cookie sheet • oven • strong glue • leather thong • earring findings

1 To form a length of twisted wire, cut double the length you require. Fold in half and grip ends in a vise.

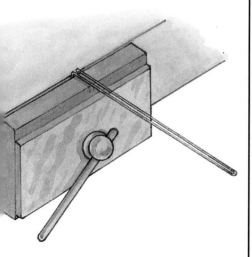

2 Open up ring of eyelet. Insert straight end into the chuck of a hand drill. Loop wire over eyelet, hold it taut, and turn drill handle until wire is evenly twisted.

3 Use twisted wire to form a circle with the loop at the top. Place circle on foil sheet and draw around inside and outside with a pencil.

4 Cut foil around outer circle with scissors and snip into inner circle at intervals. Press edge upward all around foil circle.

5 Bend more twisted wire to form a square and a circle. Lay these inside foil circle. Drop pieces of different colored plastic into each shape.

6 Lay foil on a cookie sheet. Bake in the oven at a high temperature for a few minutes (just long enough for the plastic granules to melt). Cool and glue wire circle to outside.

7 Hang pendant from leather thong. Attach earrings to findings. Glue ring to a circle of twisted wire.

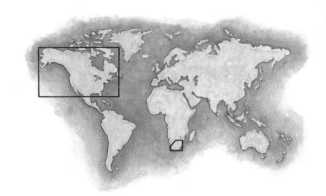

Beads with
a message

The Zulu and Swazi peoples of South Africa have developed very complex and beautiful jewelry. They use tiny glass trading beads, called *rocailles* or seed beads. The black and white Zulu bracelet (below right) has been made by winding long strings of beads around bundled grasses or leather thongs.

In Zulu culture, the colors of the beads and the way that they are arranged can be used to send messages. The love token (below left) is called a *ncwadi*. It is given by a girl to her boyfriend. Red beads mean intense love: "My heart bleeds for you." Yellow stands for jealousy, and black for anger and hurt: "My heart has become as black as the rafters of the hut, as I hear you have taken another maiden."

The Inuit and Native American tribes of North America use seed beads to make jewelry. This buffalo scarf ring (below center) is made from beads that cover part of a cow's bone.

Make a message token

You will need: paper • colored pencils • ruler • silk thread • scissors • bead loom • beading needle • beeswax block • shallow container • seed beads of different colors • large safety pin • strong glue

1 Prepare a diagram of the design you want to make by drawing several parallel lines on paper. These represent the warp threads. Color in your bead design.

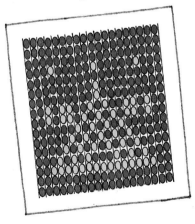

2 Estimate the length of your design and add an extra 18 inches (45 cm). Cut enough silk threads to this length for the warps. Thread your loom according to its instructions.

3 Thread a beading needle with a long double thread. Draw the thread over a beeswax block. Tie the end to the left-hand warp thread.

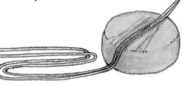

4 Put your beads in a long shallow container. "Scoop" the beads you want for your design onto the needle.

5 Pass the needle under the warp threads and press a bead up into each space between the warps.

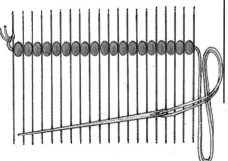

6 Bring the needle around to the right side and pass it back through the beads on the top of the work. Straighten the beads and begin the next row.

7 To finish the piece, cut the knots from the warps. Tie threads from the top end to a large safety pin and add a dot of glue. To make a fringe for the bottom, thread two warps in one needle and add 10 beads. Knot, glue, and cut off.

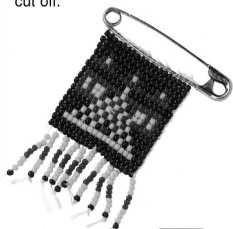

Animals, birds, and fishes

Hunters often wear the claws or teeth of animals that they have caught. In this way the hunter can demonstrate his own power or the animal's speed or strength. Sometimes model creatures are worn, as on this splendid necklace from Orissa in India (shown left). Each animal has been individually carved from wood and painted, before being threaded onto strings of dyed wooden beads.

The parrot earrings and fish earrings come from South America. Copies of local creatures are individually carved from soft wood. They are then painted and varnished before the wire earring findings are added.

Although the African necklace (below left) has been made for the tourist trade, it follows in this same tradition. The black and white claws are copies of wild animal claws, and the two giraffes have been carved and painted.

Make a necklace of creatures

These little animals are made from clay. However, if you are good at whittling, you might like to carve them from soft wood. Drill a hole right through the back of each carved animal, using the smallest drill bit, before sanding and painting them.

You will need: self-hardening clay • knife • thin wire • scissors • needle • gesso • poster paints • varnish • mixed beads • barrel clasp • needle • silk • nail polish or glue

1 Roll self-hardening clay into balls the size of marbles. Form each ball into a rough animal shape.

2 Use a knife to cut the leg shapes in half. Form details such as ears, horns, or trunk. Cut and insert small pieces of thin wire to make tails and tusks.

3 Make a hole through the back of each animal with a needle. Enlarge by gently turning needle in a circle. Leave clay to harden.

4 Paint animals with gesso and let dry; then paint with poster paints. Varnish.

5 Prepare a necklace of different colored beads (see page 7). Thread a needle with silk and knot the end. Secure with nail polish or glue. Thread one small bead and then an animal. Follow with several beads.

6 Place the thread over the necklace so that the animal hangs down where you want it. Knot to finish. Repeat with all the animals. Finish necklace with a barrel clasp.

15

MEXICO

Dancing skeletons

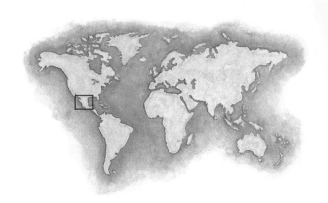

In Mexico, October 31, or Halloween, is widely celebrated as The Day of the Dead. The celebrations involve a half-serious, half-amusing approach to the subject of death. People have fun by making skeletons and skulls out of many materials. The objects they make even include items of jewelry, like these skeleton earrings, which are made entirely of silver wire.

The Grim Reaper, or figure of death, pendant is made from sections of thin tin. The metal is cut out and then shaped by scoring the back with a metal tool. This technique is called *repoussé* work. It is widely used to make many different kinds of metal jewelry.

Make your own dancing bones

You will need: tin snips • soda can • mallet • wooden board • felt-tip pen • metal file • plastic modeling material • awl • hammer • two silver wire rings • necklace and earring findings

1 With tin snips, pierce the side of can. Cut off top and bottom and cut open the cylinder.

Flatten metal on a board with a mallet.

2 Use a felt-tip pen to draw two halves of a skeleton, with scythe in its hand, on the metal. Add tabs to the legs and body. Add features and bones with felt-tip pen. Cut out with tin snips.

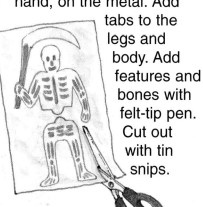

3 File edges smooth. Place each piece on plastic modeling material and pierce holes in tabs and scythe with a hammer and awl.

4 Join the two halves with a silver wire ring. Add a second ring to the scythe. Thread this ring onto a chain.

5 Make two small skeleton earrings in a similar way. Hang from silver earring findings.

Wrists, ears, and ankles

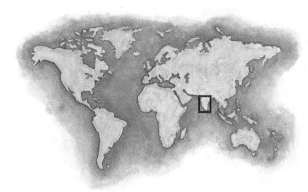

A wedding in India is an occasion for wearing special jewelry. The man who is getting married wears a decorated wristband (top left). The women wear special items of jewelry, in particular ornaments for the hands, feet, face, and hair. The gold ornament (bottom left) is worn on the forehead and attached to the hair with hooks. The nose ring (bottom right) can be slipped over the nostril, which does not need to be pierced.

In addition, hair ornaments are woven into the woman's braids. The colors are chosen to match the sari that she is wearing.

The armlet shown left center is in a different style from the wedding ornaments. It is made by the Banjara tribal people of India. Mirror disks have been embroidered onto a fabric band, and cotton tassels have been attached with cast-metal beads and findings. Decorations like this are worn around the upper arm, neck, and ankles.

Make a wedding wristband

You will need: strong glue • sparkly giftwrap ribbon • three paper balls (sold in craft shops) • a bunch of tinsel • masking tape • needle • thick embroidery cotton • string of beads

If you cannot find craft paper balls to make this wedding decoration, make your own by wrapping masking tape around pieces of crumpled newspaper.

2 Wrap a bunch of tinsel with masking tape. Bind the tape with thick embroidery cotton.

4 Add a second tinsel bunch and a string of beads.

1 Spread glue along a length of ribbon. Wind it around a paper ball so that each strand covers the edge of the strand before. Continue until the ball is covered.

3 Sew tinsel to top of wrapped ball. Sew several strands of cotton around ball to decorate.

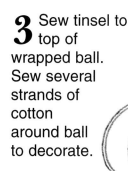

5 Repeat with two smaller paper balls. Sew the three balls onto a length of giftwrap ribbon to be tied around the wearer's wrist.

INDIA, SOUTH AMERICA, AND SOUTH AFRICA

Friendship bracelets

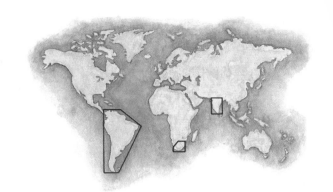

Bangles of all kinds are popular in India, where they are worn especially by married women. They can be made from gold or silver, resin, shell, ivory, or glass. Bangles like the ones shown below left are sold in the markets or bazaars, or by traveling bangle sellers.

A type of woven bracelet is popular in many parts of the world. It is easily made from scraps of wool or cotton. The bracelets are often given to someone special, so they have become known as friendship bracelets. The examples below come from South America, India, and Africa.

The colorful wire bracelet from South Africa (right) is a good example of the way in which people adapt to using new materials. It is made out of plastic-covered wires that are found inside modern telephone cables. The wires are covered in plastic of different colors so that the engineers can tell them apart. People have discovered a way of weaving these wires into many decorative items.

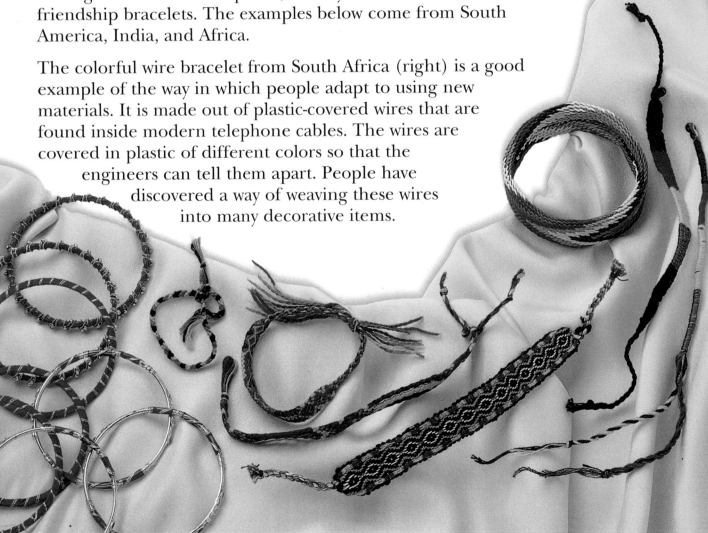

Make your own bangles

You will need: 0.8-mm wire, silver and copper • pliers • hand drill • vise • small metal eyelet or hook • plain plastic bangle • glue • colored wool or thick embroidery cotton (several colors) • thin silver or gold thread

You could use your bead loom to weave a friendship bracelet from colored wools. If you want to send a message to someone, use the traditional Zulu colors described on page 12.

Here are ideas for making two different bangles. After you have made the bangles, you might like to invent your own methods of making others.

1 Twist together some silver wire and copper wire (see page 11). Form into a ring to fit your wrist.

2 Using pliers, form each end of the wire into a hook. Twist hooks together to close bangle.

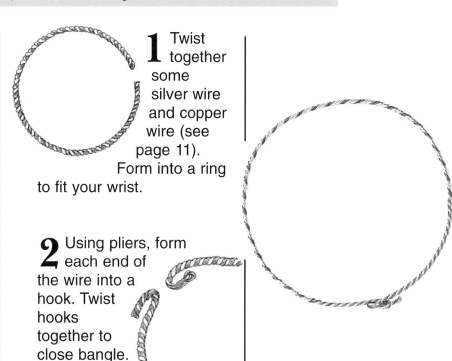

1 Use an old plain plastic bangle, or buy one from a thrift shop. Choose balls of colored wool or thick embroidery cotton. Glue the end of one color of cotton along the bangle and begin wrapping cotton over it, around the bangle.

2 Add a second color of cotton, wrapping it over the original color and its own end. Alternate colors in this way until the whole bangle is covered.

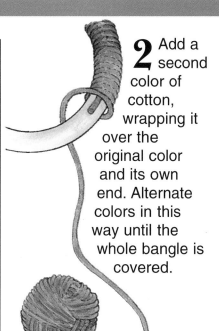

3 For extra decoration, bind thin silver or gold thread over the top.

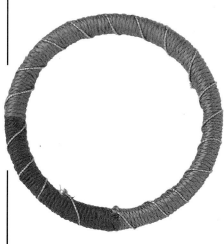

Hair decorations

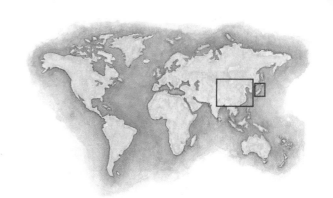

These little hair ornaments are made from molded plaster. They represent well-known characters in the traditional Peking Opera of China. They have elastic loops at the back, which hold a bunch of hair in place.

A hairstyle is a very important part of the grooming of a traditional Japanese woman, such as the one shown below. She will often need help to create the elaborate style. In order to keep it in place for several days, she sleeps with her neck on a special wooden pillow covered with a small pad. Her hair is coated with oil of camellia and kept in place with large wooden combs or long decorated hairpins.

Make Chinese hair ornaments

This method can be used to make as many identical plaster casts of the original ornament as you like. You can also make the hair ornaments into brooches by adding a safety pin instead of elastic. This could be a good way of making gifts for friends or items to sell at a local fair or school fund-raising event.

You will need: self-hardening clay • plastic modeling material • rolling pin • plaster of Paris • four wire loops • poster paints • varnish • length of round elastic

1 Form a ball of self-hardening clay into a face shape. Copy one of the characters from Chinese opera, or another character if you prefer. This will be your original. Leave to harden.

2 Roll a piece of plastic modeling material into a flat oval shape. Lay it over the original face and press gently all over. Flatten the edges against your work surface.

3 Gently ease modeling material off original and turn mold upside down. Rest on a pad of modeling material without damaging the shape.

4 Mix up plaster of Paris until it is as thick as heavy cream. Pour into mold until full. Press two wire loops into wet plaster. Leave to dry.

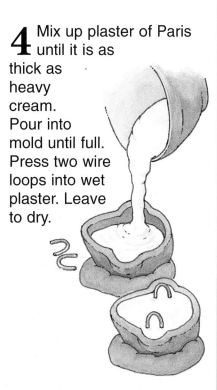

5 Ease modeling material off plaster mold. Paint and varnish. Tie elastic to both loops. Make other ornaments in the same way.

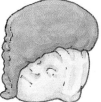

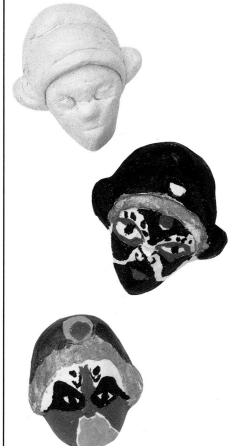

Symbols and charms

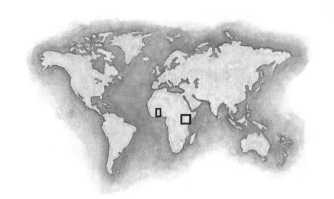

People like to wear around their necks ornaments that mean something special to them. The carved wooden pendant (below right) is a good example. It is used as a charm by the Akua tribe in Ghana. It springs from the legend of Akua, a woman who was considered barren (unable to have children) until she gave birth to a beautiful daughter. She called the child Akuaba.

The figure of Akuaba is carved from light-colored wood, which is then painted. A charm like this is often made by a husband, who gives it to his wife to help her to have children. It is also meant to make sure that her baby is beautiful. If a woman cannot have children, the charm will be buried with her when she dies. Akua fathers also give carved Akuaba dolls to their daughters to play with.

The tiny drum from Kenya (below left) is made for tourists as a symbol of Africa. It is carved from soft wood and has a leather skin. The drum is strung in the same way as a real drum.

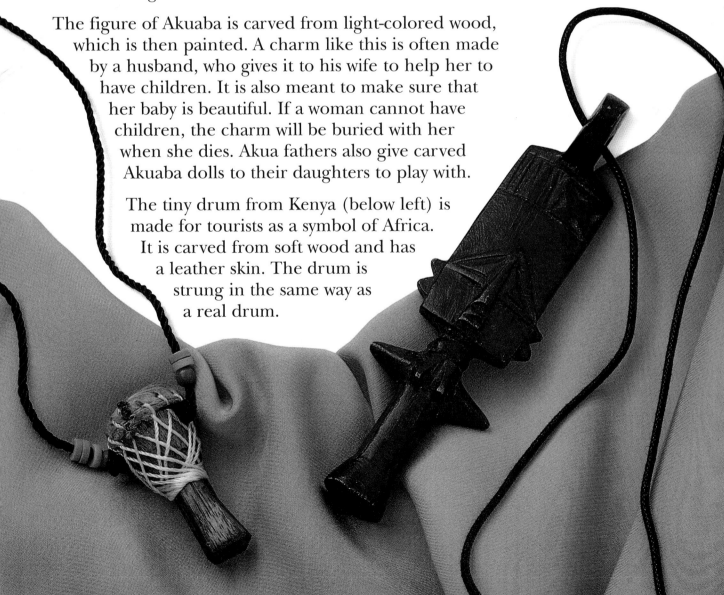

Make a tiny carved drum

If you are good at carving, you could make a doll figure like Akuaba, or some other figure or object that means something special to you.

You will need: half-inch (15-mm) dowel, 1.5 inches (35 mm) long • pencil • craft knife • chamois leather • scissors • glue • black thread • needle • length of cord • beads

1 Mark point half an inch (15 mm) from top of dowel. Draw circle a quarter inch (10 mm) across on base.

2 With a craft knife, begin to "sharpen" bottom end of dowel by slicing away the wood, until the end is the same size as the small circle.

3 Make the drum's "waist" by cutting inward from both sides at the half-inch mark.

Continue until the correct shape is formed.

4 Place the drum upside down on the chamois leather. Draw a circle slightly larger all around. Cut out leather circle with scissors. Glue to top of drum.

5 Tie black thread around loose edges of leather. Tie a second length of thread around drum's "waist" and thread the other end through a needle.

6 Bring thread up and sew downward, behind thread and leather, then down around "waist" and up again. Sew another stitch to the left of the first. Continue until you have sewn all the way around the drum head. Knot thread.

7 To hang the drum, knot the cord and beads under the threads.

Special purposes

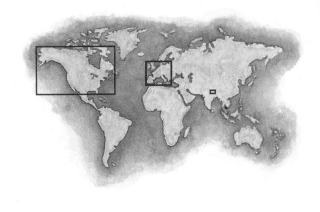

Jewelry can be used for religious purposes as well as for decorative ones. A good example is the rosary (right), which is used by Roman Catholics as an aid to prayer. It is interesting to note that the word *bead* comes from the Anglo-Saxon word for "bidden (or called) to pray."

The set of Buddhist prayer beads (below center), called a *chursa*, comes from Tibet. The beads are made of brass and are strung onto a thick coil, or hank, of cotton threads. Each side has ten beads.

The dream catcher's web shown left has quite a different use. It is made by native North Americans. Their legend says that while you sleep, your dreams will either leave you or come true. If you wear the web, or hang it near your bed, it will attract the dream spirits. Your good dreams will escape through the center of the web and become real. Your bad dreams will become trapped in the web and disappear with each new day.

Make a dream catcher

You will need: soft leather or suede • glue • large wooden curtain (or embroidery) ring • silk or cotton embroidery thread • needle • three beads • feathers • leather thong

1 Cut strips of soft leather or suede. Glue one end of a strip to the curtain ring and begin to wind the leather tightly around it, leaving no gaps. When you reach the end of the strip, glue it down. Continue with more strips until the ring is covered.

2 Knot thread and wrap it loosely around the ring, forming eight loops.

3 Using a needle, pass the thread around the inside of the ring again. Loosely knot the thread to each loop.

4 Finally, link each loop to its opposite number. Hold a bead in the center of the web and pass the needle and thread through the bead each time.

5 Tie short length of leather to finished ring. Glue beads and feathers to ends. Hang ring on leather thong.

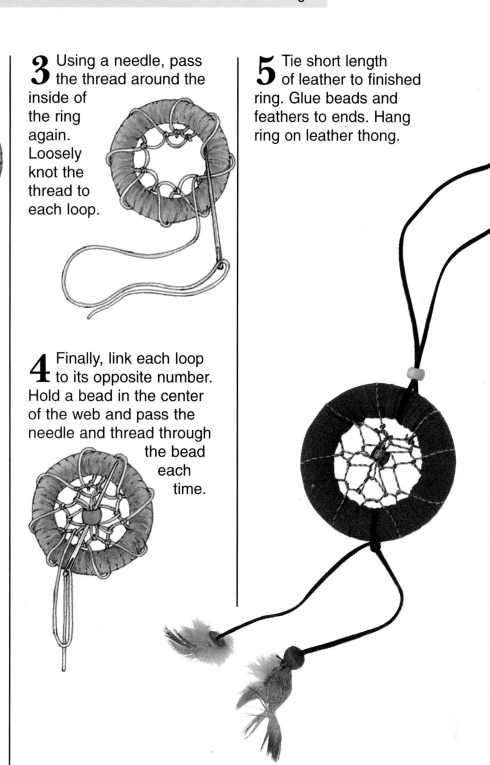

Two helpful accessories

This book contains some ideas for jewelry that you can make, but there are literally thousands of other kinds throughout the world.

It is worth making a trip to your local library to look at some of the books listed on page 30. You should be able to find many other inspiring designs to copy. A visit to a bead shop can also help you make up your own designs for jewelry.

Here are two ideas to help you become a jewelry enthusiast!

You will soon need somewhere to keep your collection of jewelry. Here is an idea for a permanent display space. It will keep your work neat and show it off well at the same time.

Threading a necklace can be a tricky business, especially if you want it to be completely symmetrical. The numbers on this threading tray will help you lay out your beads evenly and plan how the finished work will look. You can keep your spare beads and equipment in the space at the bottom end of the tray.

Create a jewelry display board

You will need:
a cork bulletin board • push pins • thick embroidery cotton or thin string • picture hook and eyelets

1 Find an old cork bulletin board. Place necklaces and bracelets on board and arrange large push pins for them to hang from.

2 For earrings, place several pins in rows opposite one another. Tie embroidery cotton or string around the pins until you have a row of parallel lines.

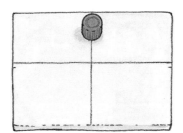

3 Leave an area where you can stick in the pins of brooches and badges.

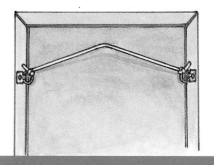

4 Stand board on a surface or hang it on the wall using eyelets and a picture hook.

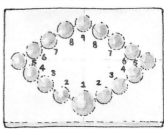

Make a bead threading tray

You will need:
a clean paint tray • polystyrene ceiling tile • craft knife • pencil • plastic bottle top • white enamel paint • felt-tip pen • glue

1 With the craft knife, cut polystyrene tile to fit on top shelf of paint tray.

2 Draw a pencil line down the middle of the tile and a second line across it, just above the middle. Using plastic bottle top, press a circle into the polystyrene, about a half inch (10 mm) from top, along middle line.

3 Make two more circles at either side and a larger one at the bottom. Draw lines between circles to form diamond shape. Fill in lines with more circles at equal distances from each other.

4 With your thumbs, press each circle into a bowl shape. Add two coats of enamel paint. Number bowls with felt-tip pen as shown. Glue tile onto paint tray.

Useful information

Supply stores

Magic Novelty Company
308 Dyckman Street
New York, NY 10034
(212) 304-2777
(hoops, posts, wires, chains, etc. — catalog available)

Sheru Bead and
Jewelry Enterprises
49 West 38th Street
New York, NY 10018
(212) 730-0766
(beads, clasps, crystals, rhinestones, etc. — catalog available)

Look in your local telephone book or *Yellow Pages* for other jewelry supply stores.

Associations

Fashion Jewelry Association
of America
3 Davol Square, Unit 135
Providence, RI 02903

Independent Jewelers
Organization
2 Railroad Place
Westport, CT 06880

Jewelers of America
1185 6th Avenue, 30th floor
New York, NY 10036

Jewelers' Book Club
Chilton Way
Radnor, PA 19089

Jewelry Information Center
8 West 19th Street, 4th floor
New York, NY 10011

Books

Making Jewelry:

The Art and Craft of Jewelry,
by Janet Fitch
(Chronicle Books, 1994)

Bead It! A Complete Jewelry Kit,
by Lara R. Bergen
(Putnam, 1994)

The Book of Jewelry: Create Your Own Jewelry with Beads, Clay, Papier-mâché, Fabric and Other Everyday Items,
by Jo Moody
(Simon & Schuster, 1994)

Jewelry (Rainy Day Arts and Crafts),
by Denny A. Robson
(Watts, 1993)

Jewelry Craft Made Easy,
by Bernada French
(Gembooks, 1993)

Jewelry Crafts (Fresh Start),
by Barrie Caldecott
(Watts, 1992)

Jewelry Making for Beginners,
by Edward J. Soukup
(Gembooks, 1973)

Make Your Own Friendship Bracelets
(Troll Associates, 1993)

History of Jewelry:

Ancient Egyptian Jewelry,
by Carol Andrews
(Abrams, 1991)

Greek and Roman Jewelry,
by Reynold A. Higgins
(University of California Press, 1980)

A History of Jewelry,
by Joan A. Evans
(Dover, 1989)

Indian Jewelry of the American Southwest,
by William A. Turnbaugh and Sarah P. Turnbaugh
(Schiffer, 1989)

Jewelry: Seven Thousand Years,
edited by Hugh Tait
(Abrams, 1991)

Jewels in Spain,
by Priscilla E. Muller
(Hispanic Society, 1972)

Glossary

adorn To clothe or decorate someone or something.

Anglo-Saxon One of the peoples who lived in Britain before the Normans invaded from France in the eleventh century.

bazaar A market in an Oriental country such as India or Egypt.

Buddhist A follower of the religion founded by Gautama Buddha in India.

chamois leather Soft leather from a sheep, goat, or deer.

charm An object that is believed to have magical power.

chuck The part of a drill or lathe that grips.

evil eye A look or stare that is believed to do harm to a person.

finding A fixing for jewelry, such as a hook, a ring, an earring hook, or a stud.

gauge A standard measure of thickness or texture.

Grim Reaper A name for the figure of death, who is often pictured with a scythe.

hide The skin of an animal.

ingot A piece of raw metal that is ready to be worked.

Liberty-style A design that has been made popular by Liberty, a famous London department store.

pendant An ornament that is worn on a chain or leather thong around the neck.

resin A kind of gum which is made from the sap of plants and trees.

rosary A chain of beads used by Roman Catholics to help them say a series of prayers.

sari A long piece of silk or cotton that is worn by Indian women. It is wrapped around the body.

scythe An old-fashioned curved knife for cutting crops.

symmetrical Exactly the same on both sides.

versatile Able to be used in many different ways.

Index

Additional photograph:
page 22 (bottom), Alain Evrard, Robert Harding Picture Library.

The wire bracelet shown on page 20 (far right) was made by Mandoda Matola.